Crafting with Felt

LEISURE ARTS, INC. • Little Rock, Arkansas

Phone Cases

SHOPPING LIST

☐ Scraps of felt in assorted colors (we used tan and brown for the bear; light pink, dark pink and blue for the pig; yellow, orange and brown for the lion; black, green and pink for the frog)

☐ Embroidery floss – brown, light pink, yellow, green, and black

☐ Embroidery needle

☐ $^5/_8$" diameter hook & loop fastener dots

☐ Two $^5/_8$" diameter wiggle eyes for frog

☐ Tracing paper

☐ Craft glue

To make Bear Phone Case:

1. Trace the bear patterns onto the tracing paper and cut out. Use the patterns to cut two phone sleeves, two arms and a nose from the brown felt; and two ears, two eyes, a muzzle and a belly from the tan felt.
2. Glue the facial pieces and belly to a brown phone sleeve. Using a straight stitch (see page 32) and 5 strands of brown floss, stitch three "claws" on one of the arms.
3. Stack the two phone sleeve pieces, wrong sides together. Place arms on bear and pin. Hands should overlap with clawed hand on top. Using a blanket stitch (see page 32) and 5 strands of brown floss, sew around the sides and bottom to attach the layers to each other. At the top, sew only the front phone sleeve.
4. Glue the hook & loop fastener dots between the hands to hold together.

Finished size: approximately 3¾" wide x 5¼" high

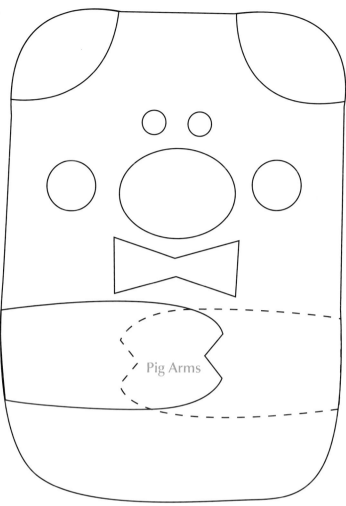

Pig Patterns

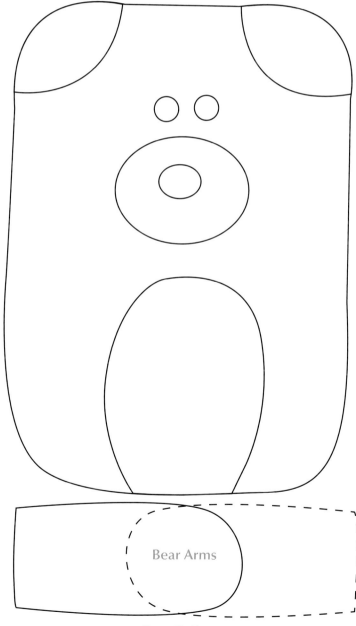

Bear Patterns

To make Pig Phone Case:

1. Trace the pig patterns onto the tracing paper and cut out. Use the patterns to cut two phone sleeves and two arms from the light pink felt; two ears, two cheeks and a nose from the dark pink felt; and two eyes and a bowtie from the blue felt.
2. Glue the facial pieces and bowtie to a light pink phone sleeve. Using 3 strands of light pink floss and a straight stitch (see page 32), stitch nostrils in the nose.
3. Stack the two phone sleeve pieces, wrong sides together. Place arms on pig and pin. Hands should overlap. Using a blanket stitch (see page 32) and 4 strands of light pink floss, sew around the sides and bottom to attach the layers to each other. At the top, sew only the front phone sleeve.
4. Glue the hook & loop fastener dots between the hands to hold together.

Finished size: approximately 3¾" wide x 5¼" high

Continued on page 4

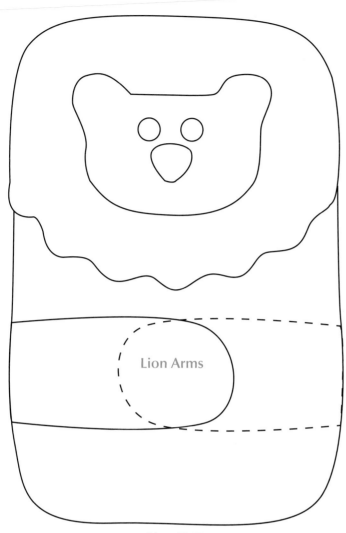

Lion Patterns

To make Frog Phone Case:

1. Trace the frog patterns onto the tracing paper and cut out. Use the patterns to cut two phone sleeves from the black felt; a frog and two arms from the green felt; and a tongue from the pink felt.

2. Using 6 strands of black floss, stem stitch (see page 32) a mouth on the frog. Glue the tongue and eyes in place. Glue the frog to a black phone sleeve.

3. Stack the two phone sleeve pieces, wrong sides together. Place arms on frog and pin. Hands should overlap. Using a blanket stitch (see page 32) and 6 strands of green floss, sew around the sides and bottom to attach the layers to each other. At the top, sew only the front phone sleeve.

4. Glue the hook & loop fastener dots between the hands to hold together.

Finished size: approximately 3¾" wide x 5¼" high

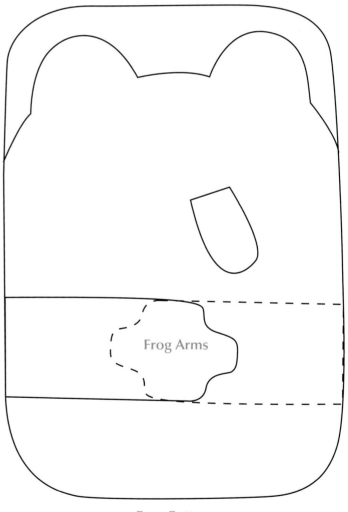

Frog Patterns

To make Lion Phone Case:

1. Trace the lion patterns onto the tracing paper and cut out. Use the patterns to cut two phone sleeves, two arms and a face from the yellow felt; a mane from the orange felt; and two eyes and a nose from the brown felt.

2. Glue the facial and mane pieces to a yellow phone sleeve. Using a straight stitch (see page 32) and 6 strands of brown floss, stitch whiskers behind the nose before gluing into place. Using a straight stitch and 6 strands of yellow floss, stitch three "claws" on one of the arms.

3. Stack the two phone sleeve pieces, wrong sides together. Place arms on lion and pin into place. Hands should overlap with clawed hand on top. Using a blanket stitch (see page 32) and 4 strands of yellow floss, sew around the sides and bottom to attach the layers to each other. At the top, sew only the front phone sleeve.

4. Glue the hook & loop fastener dots between the hands to hold together.

Finished size: approximately 3¾" wide x 5¼" high

Door Signs

SHOPPING LIST

- ☐ Large stiffened felt base shapes (we used a 13" purple flower, a 13" red star and a 12" green butterfly)
- ☐ Assorted adhesive-backed felt letters (ours are 1" high)
- ☐ Assorted adhesive-backed felt shapes to personalize
- ☐ Gold and silver sequins for Star Door Sign
- ☐ Jewel stones for Butterfly Door Sign
- ☐ Two ½" diameter wiggle eyes for Butterfly Door Sign
- ☐ Two wooden spring clothespins for Butterfly Door Sign
- ☐ Hot pink acrylic paint and paintbrush for Butterfly Door Sign
- ☐ Craft glue

To make Flower Door Sign:
Arrange letters on flower base as desired; adhere to base. Arrange shapes (we used a peace sign, hearts, a flower and leaf, and a pair of flip flops) in remaining space; adhere to base.

To make Star Door Sign:
Arrange letters on star base as desired; adhere to the base. Arrange shapes (we used black, yellow and white stars, and a guitar) in remaining space; adhere to the base. Glue sequins to base.

To make Butterfly Door Sign:
Paint clothespins; glue to butterfly base. Arrange letters on base as desired; adhere to the base. Arrange shapes (we used two flowers and three butterflies) in remaining space; adhere to the base. Glue jewels and eyes in place.

Bulletin Board

SHOPPING LIST

☐ Memo board with cork and dry-erase sides (ours measures 23" x 17")

☐ 9" x 12" sheets of adhesive-backed felt in 4 colors/patterns – (we used black, orange, white and tiger-stripe)

☐ White adhesive-backed felt letters (ours are 1" high)

☐ Assorted adhesive-backed felt shapes (we used a football, baseball, soccer ball and basketball)

To make Bulletin Board:

1. Measure opening for cork side of memo board (ours measures 11½" x 16½"). Divide each measurement in half. Cut four pieces of contrasting felt to these measurements. Adhere the felt pieces to the cork, tucking outer edges underneath frame if possible. Felt should not overlap in the center; small gaps are okay and will be covered.

2. Cut two ⅝" wide strips of a third felt pattern/color that are the same height as the previously cut pieces. Starting at the top, adhere one strip to the cork board, covering the gap between the top quarters. Repeat with the second ⅝" wide strip on bottom.

3. Cut a 2¾" strip of the same felt used in Step 2 by the width of the cork side. Cut a 3¼" strip of a fourth pattern/color felt the width of the cork side. Layer and adhere the felt strips to cork board.

4. Adhere letters and shapes on the board as desired.

Pennants & Photo Frame

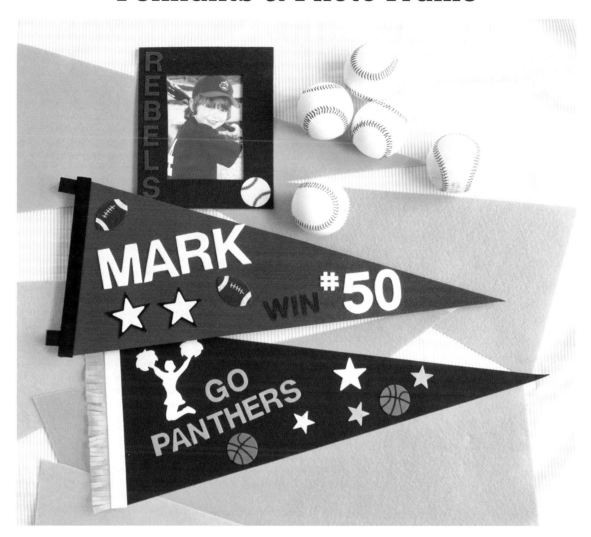

SHOPPING LIST

☐ Stiffened felt pennants (we used red and navy)

☐ 9" x 12" adhesive-backed felt sheets (we used black and white)

☐ Assorted adhesive-backed felt letters and numbers (ours are 1" and 2" high)

☐ Assorted adhesive-backed felt shapes (we used a football, basketball, baseball, cheerleader and stars)

☐ Tracing paper

☐ 1½" x 9" strip of felt for fringed pennant

☐ Craft glue for fringed pennant

To make Pennants:

1. Arrange letters, numbers and shapes on pennant as desired. Remove backing and adhere letters, numbers and shapes to the pennant.

2. To trim the pennant with tabs, cut a ¾" wide adhesive-backed felt strip the same height as the pennant. Cut two ¾" x 2" adhesive-backed felt strips. Matching the short ends, fold the 2" strips in half. Adhere the long ¾" wide strip to the pennant end, sandwiching the folded strips between the pennant and the strip.

3. To trim the pennant with fringe, make ¾" deep cuts ¼" apart on the long edge of the 9" fringe strip. Cut a ¾" wide adhesive-backed felt strip the same height as the pennant. Glue the fringe strip to the pennant end. Adhere the ¾" wide strip over the fringe.

Finished size: 22" x 9" excluding fringe

To make Photo Frame:

Cut a 3½" x 5½" opening in a 7" x 8½" sheet of stiffened felt. Adhere desired letters and shapes to the frame.

Finished size: 7" x 8½"

Tote Bag

SHOPPING LIST

- □ 12" x 18" sheet of light blue stiffened felt
- □ Assorted adhesive-backed felt shapes
  (we used 3 flowers, 3 leaves and 1 bee)
- □ Scrap lime green adhesive-backed felt
- □ Embroidery floss
  (we used black, light blue, pink and yellow)
- □ Embroidery needle
- □ Assorted buttons (we used two pink ½" diameter and
  one yellow 5/8" diameter buttons)
- □ Two 12" lengths of white 5/8" wide twill tape
- □ Disappearing fabric marker
- □ Spray bottle
- □ Craft glue

To make Tote Bag:

1. Cut one 2" x 18" strip and two 6" squares from light blue felt sheet. Using the blanket stitch (see page 32) and 2 strands of light blue floss, sew the long side of the felt strip to three edges of a felt square. Repeat with the other felt square to create tote. Crease the strip at the bottom corners of the bag.
2. Sew buttons in center of flowers with 4 strands of yellow or pink floss.
3. For stems, cut three ¼" x 2½" lengths of lime green felt. Arrange flowers, stems and leaves on tote front; adhere. Secure with glue if desired.
4. Adhere bee to tote, securing with glue if desired. Very lightly freehand draw the flight path on the tote with the marker. Using the running stitch (see page 32), stitch the flight path with 3 strands of black floss. If any marker line is visible, carefully erase by spritzing with water.
5. Sew twill tape handles inside the tote upper corners with 4 strands of blue floss.

Finished size: 6" x 6" x 2" excluding handles

Owl Pin

SHOPPING LIST

- □ Scrap of hot pink stiffened felt
- □ Scraps of felt (lime green, white and orange)
- □ 5" of light blue ¼" wide baby rickrack
- □ Two ¼" diameter black buttons
- □ Black thread
- □ ¾" long metal bar pin back
- □ Tracing paper
- □ Craft glue

To make Owl Pin:

1. Trace the patterns onto the tracing paper and cut out. Use the patterns to cut owl from hot pink felt, two wings from lime green felt, two eyes from white felt and beak from orange felt.
2. Place eyes on owl body. Using black thread, sew the buttons and eyes to owl. Glue the beak into place.
3. Cut rickrack to three 1½" lengths. Glue across the owl's belly, trimming edges. Glue wings to owl sides. Glue pin to back.

Finished size: approximately 2" tall

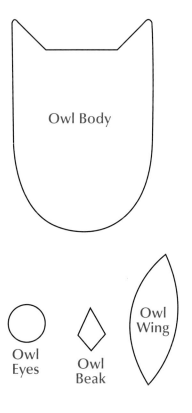

Owl Body

Owl Eyes

Owl Beak

Owl Wing

Cupcake Pin

Shown on page 8.

SHOPPING LIST

- ☐ Scraps of pink and tan felt
- ☐ Red embroidery floss
- ☐ Embroidery needle
- ☐ 7/16" diameter red shank-style button
- ☐ ¾" long metal bar pin back
- ☐ Tracing paper
- ☐ Craft glue

To make Cupcake Pin:

1. Trace the patterns onto the tracing paper and cut out. Use the patterns to cut two cupcakes from tan felt and two frostings from pink felt.
2. Matching edges, glue the cupcakes together.
3. Stitch around the edge of one frosting piece with a running stitch (see page 32) and 3 strands of floss, attaching button at top. Embellish with French knots using 4 strands of floss. Matching edges, glue frosting pieces together, sandwiching cupcake in between. Glue pin to back.

Finished size: approximately 2" tall

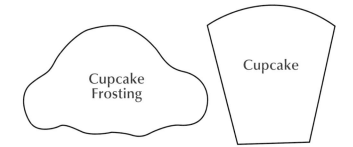

Bluebird Pin

Shown on page 8.

SHOPPING LIST

- ☐ Scraps of blue, light blue and orange felt
- ☐ Light blue and black embroidery floss
- ☐ Embroidery needle
- ☐ ¾" long metal bar pin back
- ☐ Tracing paper
- ☐ Craft glue

To make Bluebird Pin:

1. Trace the patterns onto the tracing paper and cut out. Use the patterns to cut two bodies from light blue felt, a wing from blue felt and a beak from orange felt.
2. Matching edges, use a running stitch (see page 32) and 3 strands of light blue floss to sew around edges of body, catching beak in stitches. Make a black French knot using 4 strands of black floss.
3. Glue wing to body front, leaving the wing tip unglued. Glue pin to back.

Finished size: approximately 2" tall

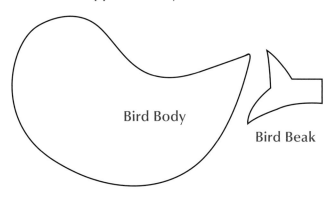

Topiary

SHOPPING LIST

☐ Large coffee mug
☐ Floral foam, cut to fill mug
☐ 5" diameter foam ball
☐ 12" x ³/₁₆" diameter dowel
☐ Green acrylic paint
☐ Paintbrush
☐ 9" x 12" sheets of felt – one light green, two medium green, one dark green
☐ ¼" diameter orange plastic beads (we used 10)
☐ 16" length of ³/₈" wide green ribbon
☐ Tracing paper
☐ Low temp glue gun with glue sticks

To make Topiary:

1. Trace the circle pattern onto the tracing paper and cut out. Use the pattern to cut circles from felt sheets–24 light, 24 medium and 20 dark green circles.

2. Wrap one sheet of medium green felt over floral foam to cover top. Fit the covered foam into the mug snugly, trimming felt as needed. Cut a slit in the top center of the felt for the dowel. Cut a slit in the center of one light green circle. Center circle over slit and glue into place.

3. Paint the dowel. Push the dowel into floral foam through the slits until it touches the bottom of the mug. Place foam ball on dowel, pushing the ball onto the dowel for about 3".

4. Starting with the dark green circles near the dowel, overlap and glue the circles to the foam ball. Continue with the medium green and light green circles, placing the last light green circle directly atop the ball.

5. Glue the orange beads to the topiary. Tie ribbon around dowel, trimming ends as desired.

Finished size: approximately 15" tall

Circle

Finger Puppets

For the One-eyed Monster:

1. Trace the puppet patterns onto the tracing paper and cut out. Use the patterns to cut the body and back pieces from felt. Using a thin line of glue on the edge of the back piece, adhere it to the body.
2. Use the patterns to cut out spots, eye pieces and mouth pieces. Glue pieces to body as desired.
3. For each antenna, coil both ends of a 4" chenille stem piece until it measures 2" long. Glue the bottom coil to the back of the body, then glue pom-pom to cover the top coil.

For the Bowtie Monster:

1. Trace the puppet patterns onto the tracing paper and cut out. Use the patterns to cut the body and back pieces from felt. Using a thin line of glue on the edge of the back piece, adhere it to the body.
2. Use the patterns to cut out hair, teeth, belly and bowtie. Cut ½" slits into a long edge of the hair piece. Glue pieces to body as desired.
3. Glue wiggle eyes to body. Cut small pieces of black yarn (ours are between ¾" and 1" in length) and glue to face for eyebrows and mouth.

Finished size: approximately 4" x 5" each

Bowtie Monster

One-eyed Monster

Puppet Back

Bowtie Monster Hair

Bird Pincushion

Fig. 1

To make Bird Pincushion:

1. Trace the patterns onto the tracing paper and cut out. Use the patterns to cut two bodies from hot pink felt, two wings from houndstooth check felt (one in reverse), two eyes from white felt and a beak from orange felt.

2. Glue one wing to each body piece. If desired, leave the wing tips unglued. Centering a button on an eye circle, sew an eye to each body piece with black thread.

3. Matching raw edges and leaving a 1" opening at the bottom, use a running stitch (see page 32) to sew around the body with pink thread using an 1/8" seam allowance, securing both the beak and looped ribbon tail in the stitching. Stuff body with fiberfill. Stitch closed.

4. Uncoil the largest part of a paper clip, leaving the smaller "foot" (see **Fig. 1**). Push the uncoiled end between the body pieces into the center bottom of the bird's body. Repeat with second paper clip. Glue to secure.

5. Push one straight pin into each button eye.

Finished size: approximately 6" tall

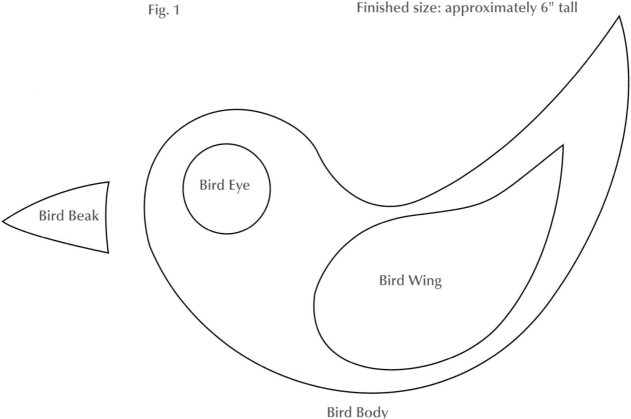

Bird Eye

Bird Beak

Bird Wing

Bird Body

CELEBR

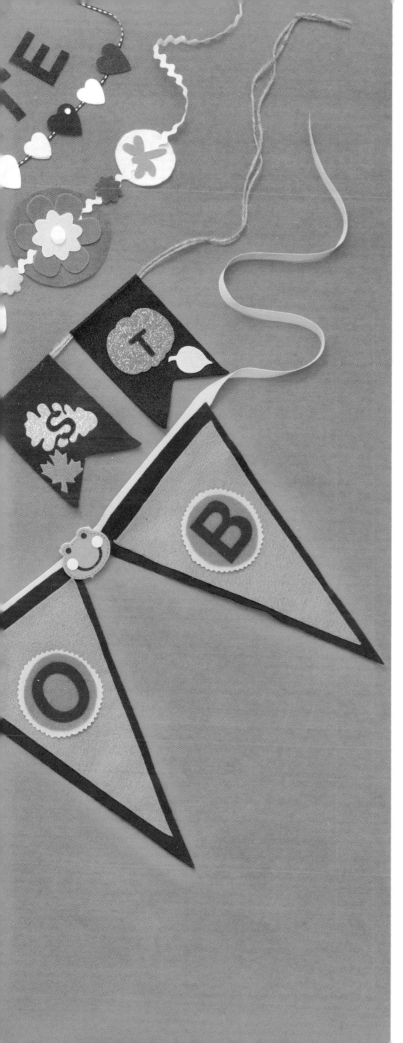

Hearts Banner

To make Hearts Banner:

1. Choose two identical hearts. Lay one face down on work surface and remove backing. Starting at least 12" from one end and keeping ribbon flat, lay ribbon across heart. Peel backing from matching heart, line up edges with first heart and adhere. Additionally secure with craft glue if desired.

2. Repeat along ribbon length. Glue additional stones to hearts if desired.

Flowers Banner

To make Flowers Banner:

1. Trace the large and small circle patterns on pages 18-19 (matching the dashed lines) onto tracing paper and cut out. Use the patterns to cut circles from felt (we used 4 large and 5 small).

2. Starting at least 12" from one end and keeping rickrack flat, lay rickrack across a small circle; secure with craft glue. Center a small flower on a medium flower, then adhere to circle, reinforcing with craft glue.

3. Choose two identical small flowers. Lay one face down on work surface and remove backing. Keeping rickrack flat, lay rickrack across flower. Peel backing from matching flower, line up edges with first flower and adhere. Additionally secure with craft glue if desired.

Continued on page 18

Flowers Banner, continued

4. Keeping rickrack flat, lay rickrack across a large circle; secure with craft glue. Center a medium shape (flower, butterfly or dragonfly) on a large flower, then adhere to circle, reinforcing with craft glue.

5. Repeat Step 3.
6. Repeat Steps 2-5, alternating medium shapes as desired. Glue pom-poms to flower centers as desired.

Harvest Banner

SHOPPING LIST

☐ 9" x 12" sheets of felt in brown, yellow and red
☐ Assorted adhesive-backed felt shapes (we used leaves and pumpkins, some with glitter)
☐ Assorted adhesive-backed felt letters (we used 1" high)
☐ Desired length of jute, doubled
☐ Tracing paper
☐ Craft glue

To make Harvest Banner:

1. Trace the pattern onto the tracing paper and cut out. Use the pattern to cut flags from felt (we used 3 brown, 2 yellow and 2 red).

2. Starting at least 12" from one end, fold top ¼" of a brown flag over the doubled jute strand; secure with craft glue. Continue attaching flags in brown-yellow-red pattern, keeping approximately 1" between flags, until all are attached.

3. Adhere shapes to the flags as desired. Adhere a letter to the center of each large shape. Reinforce with craft glue if desired.

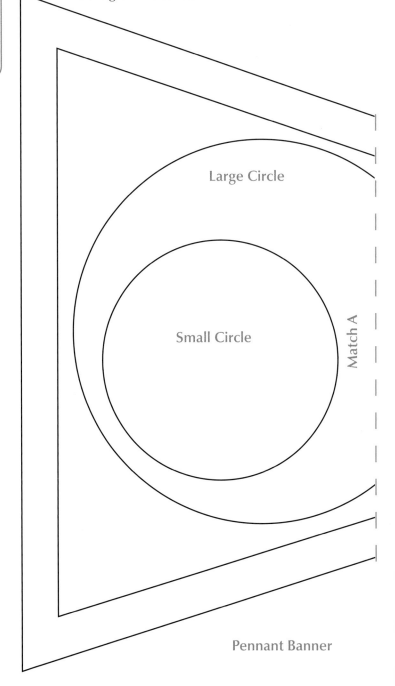

Large Circle

Small Circle

Match A

Harvest Banner

Pennant Banner

Pennant Banner

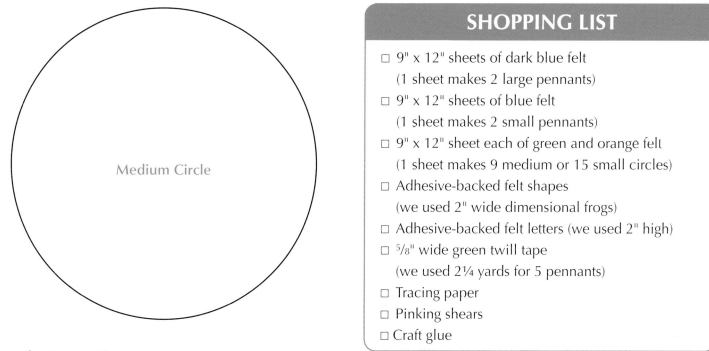

Medium Circle

- ☐ 9" x 12" sheets of dark blue felt
  (1 sheet makes 2 large pennants)
- ☐ 9" x 12" sheets of blue felt
  (1 sheet makes 2 small pennants)
- ☐ 9" x 12" sheet each of green and orange felt
  (1 sheet makes 9 medium or 15 small circles)
- ☐ Adhesive-backed felt shapes
  (we used 2" wide dimensional frogs)
- ☐ Adhesive-backed felt letters (we used 2" high)
- ☐ $5/8$" wide green twill tape
  (we used 2¼ yards for 5 pennants)
- ☐ Tracing paper
- ☐ Pinking shears
- ☐ Craft glue

To make Pennant Banner:

1. Trace the patterns onto the tracing paper (matching the dashed lines) and cut out. Use the patterns to cut pennants and circles from felt (we used one set per letter: large dark blue pennant, small blue pennant, medium green circle cut with pinking shears, and small orange circle).

2. Trace the outline of adhesive shape onto tracing paper and cut out. Use the pattern to cut a shape from scrap felt for each adhesive-back shape.

3. To make the pennant, center a small blue pennant over a large dark blue pennant and glue into place. Adhere a letter to the center of an orange circle, then glue the orange circle to a green circle. Center green circle on pennant and glue. Repeat for each letter of name.

4. Starting at least 18" from one end, glue pennant to twill. Continue attaching pennants to twill, keeping approximately ¾" between pennants, until all are attached.

5. Peel backing from felt shape and adhere between pennants, then glue plain felt shape to back. Continue attaching shapes between pennants until all are attached.

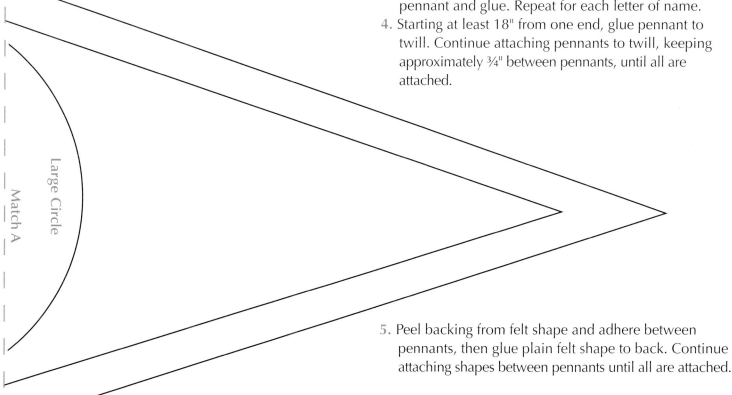

Large Circle

Match A

Owl Pillow

To make Owl Pillow:

1. Trace the patterns (below and page 22) onto the tracing paper and cut out. Use the patterns to cut two bodies from gray felt, four large wings and brow from dark blue felt, and two small wings and a beak from orange felt.

2. Matching raw edges of the body pieces and using a $1/8"$ seam allowance, machine stitch around the sides and top of the owl. Leave bottom open.

3. Pin the brow piece at top of owl. Place beak on face, tucking top under brow. Glue the beak to the owl. Use 3 strands of floss to hand sew the brow to the owl with a running stitch (see page 32). Adhere brown rings to the owl and work straight stitches (see page 32) around the rings with 3 strands of floss. Adhere white circles, small flower shapes and pom-poms to the owl.

4. Cut 1" x 9" strips of felt for chest (4 blue and 2 green). Cut fringe along one long side of each strip, ¾" deep and approximately ¼" apart. Approximately 3" from the bottom, hand stitch the bottom blue strip across the owl's belly in an arc, slightly gathering the felt. Repeat with each strip, overlapping the previous row and maintaining the same arc. Trim sides as necessary.

5. Matching raw edges of two large wings, use 3 strands of floss to hand stitch around the edges with a running stitch. Glue small orange wing in center of large wing. Repeat for second wing. Sew tops of wings to owl, reinforcing with glue if desired.

6. Stuff owl with fiberfill. Using a ¼" seam allowance, sew bottom closed.

7. For feet, fold large flower shapes in half, sticky sides together. Glue to bottom of owl.

Finished size: approximately 8" x 11"

Owl Beak

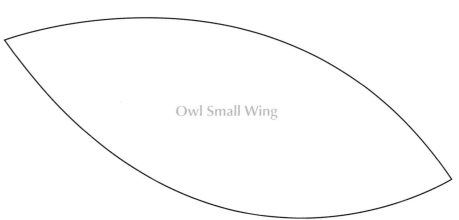

Owl Small Wing

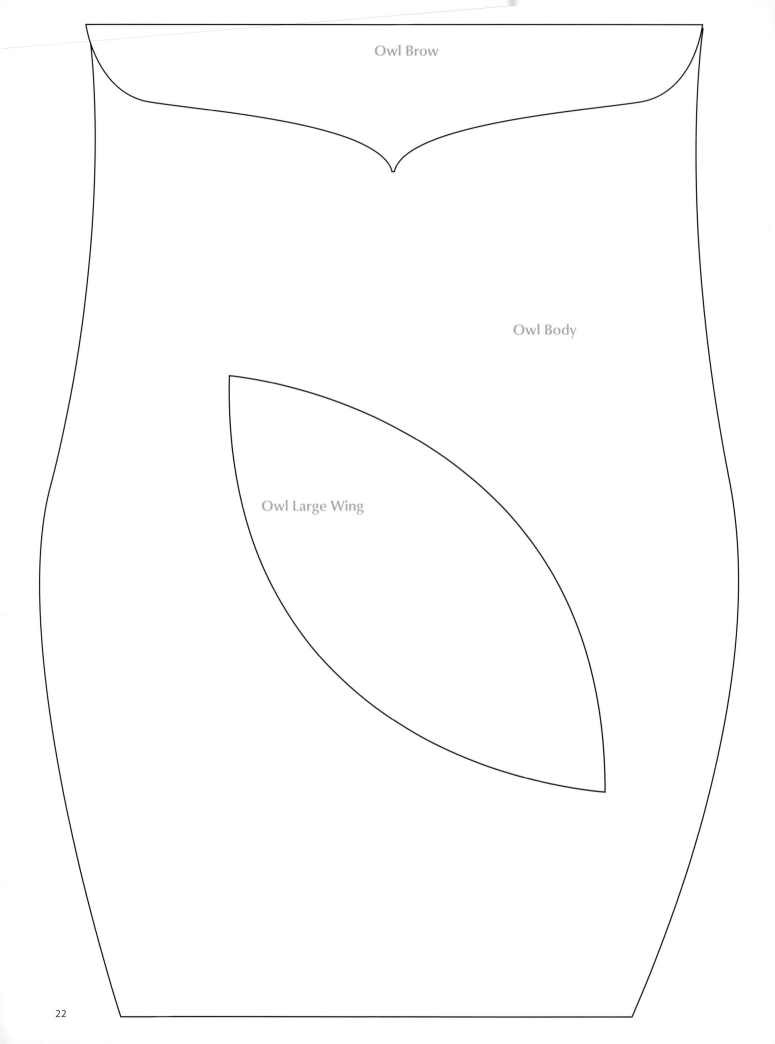

Owl Brow

Owl Body

Owl Large Wing

Headbands

SHOPPING LIST

- □ Stretchy headband
- □ Adhesive-backed felt shape
  (we used a ladybug, an owl and a cat)
- □ Scraps of felt for backing
- □ Tracing paper
- □ Craft glue

To make Headbands:

1. Trace the felt shape onto the tracing paper and cut out. Use the pattern to cut a backing from coordinating felt scrap.
2. Lay plain felt shape on flat surface. Lay headband seam over felt shape and secure with glue.
3. Remove backing from adhesive felt shape, align edges and adhere to plain felt shape.

Felt-Wrapped Wreath

SHOPPING LIST

- ☐ 10" diameter foam wreath
- ☐ Thin batting
- ☐ Assorted 9" x 12" sheets of felt in coordinating colors (we used 8 fall colors)
- ☐ 1¼" diameter button
- ☐ Embroidery floss to coordinate with felt
- ☐ Embroidery needle
- ☐ 26-gauge wire
- ☐ Wire cutters
- ☐ Low temp glue gun with glue sticks

To make Felt-Wrapped Wreath:

1. Cut batting into 3" wide strips. Wrap strips around wreath, securing with glue as necessary. Repeat for a second layer.
2. Cut felt sheets into 12" strips (we used 33 strips in all, both 1" and 1½" wide). Wrap overlapping strips around wreath, securing with glue in back. Continue until wreath is covered, trimming strip ends as necessary.
3. For the bow, cut a 3" x 12" strip of felt. Form strip into loop with ends tucked under center of loop, overlapping slightly. Twist wire tightly around center of loop to form bow, trimming excess wire with cutters.
4. Sew floss through button holes, knotting in back. Glue button to bow. Glue bow to wreath.

Finished size: 10¼" diameter

Mum Kid's Shoes

SHOPPING LIST

- ☐ Pair of kid's shoes
- ☐ Two 2½" squares of lime green felt
- ☐ Two 2½" x 6¼" pieces of yellow felt
- ☐ Two 2½" x 3½" pieces of hot pink felt
- ☐ Low temp glue gun with glue sticks

To make the Mum Kid's Shoes:

1. Fold a lime green felt square in half, gluing edges closed. Make fringe cuts into the fold approximately ¾" deep, about ¼" apart.
2. Fold a yellow felt piece in half, long sides together, gluing edges closed. Make fringe cuts into the fold approximately ¾" deep, about ¼" apart.
3. Repeat Step 2 with a hot pink felt piece.
4. For the mum center, coil lime green felt piece onto itself, securing the uncut bottom edges with glue. Wrap the mum center with yellow felt piece, followed by the hot pink piece, gluing the bottom edges as necessary.
5. Repeat Steps 1-4 with second set of felt pieces. Glue flowers to shoes.

Finished size: approximately 2¾" diameter flowers

Begonia Flip Flops

SHOPPING LIST

- ☐ Pair of flip flops
- ☐ 9" x 12" sheet of pink and white polka dot felt
- ☐ White embroidery floss
- ☐ Embroidery needle
- ☐ Tracing paper
- ☐ Craft glue

To make the Begonia Flip Flops:

1. For the flower centers, cut a strip of felt ¾" x 6". Cut the strip diagonally, from corner to corner, to create two triangles. Beginning at the midpoint, cut gentle waves along the long angled felt edge. Starting with the point and gluing as necessary, roll the triangle to form the flower center.
2. Trace the begonia patterns onto the tracing paper and cut out. Use the patterns to cut two large begonias and two small begonias from the felt. Place each small begonia in center of a large begonia; glue into place.
3. Place a center on a begonia. Glue into place, adding a ring of glue around the bottom of the center and pushing the petals up around the center.
4. Use floss to sew begonias to flip flops.

Finished size: approximately 2½" diameter flowers

Geranium Flats

SHOPPING LIST

- ☐ Pair of shoes
- ☐ 9" x 12" sheet each of yellow and green felt
- ☐ Tracing paper
- ☐ Low temp glue gun with glue sticks

To make the Geranium Flats:

1. Trace the patterns onto the tracing paper and cut out. Use the patterns to cut six leaves from the green felt plus two bases and 36 petals from the yellow felt.
2. Lay a yellow petal on a flat surface. Place a small dot of glue on the edge. Fold the petal in half and pinch, closing one side of the petal (see **Fig. 1**). Repeat to make a total of 18 petals.
3. Glue six petals together, creating a circular shape floret. Repeat to make a total of three florets.
4. Arrange florets on a yellow base and glue to complete the geranium.
5. Repeat Step 2 with the green leaves, making a total of three leaves. Arrange the leaves beneath the geranium and glue to the base.
6. Repeat Steps 2-5 to make another geranium. Glue the geraniums to the shoes.

Finished size: approximately 4" diameter flowers, including leaves

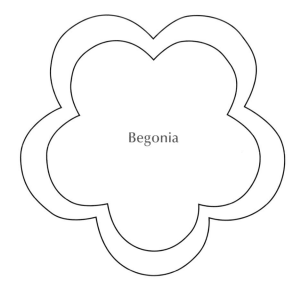

Begonia

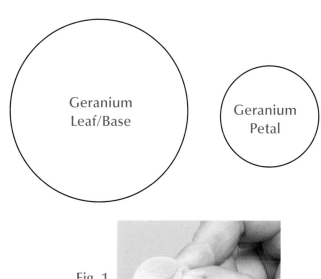

Geranium Leaf/Base

Geranium Petal

Fig. 1

Rose Cupcake

SHOPPING LIST

- ☐ 9" x 12" sheet each of yellow and hot pink felt
- ☐ Scrap of green felt
- ☐ ½" diameter yellow pom-poms (we used 13)
- ☐ ³/₈" diameter pearl bead
- ☐ Cupcake liner
- ☐ Tracing paper
- ☐ Craft glue

To make the Cupcake:

1. Trace the pattern onto the tracing paper and cut out. Use the patterns to cut two leaves from green felt.

2. To make the cupcake base, cut a 1" x 12" strip of yellow felt. Coil felt on itself, gluing into place. Continue cutting strips and coiling until the coil covers the bottom of the cupcake liner while sitting in it. Trim ends if necessary. Glue base to liner.

3. Cut a 2" circle of hot pink felt. Starting at edge, cut toward the center in a spiral (see **Fig. 1**). Starting with the center, wind the spiral on itself to create the rose center, securing with glue.

4. Cut a 5" circle of hot pink felt. Cut toward the center in a spiral, as in Step 3. Then cut waves in the outer edge of the spiral for "petals." Glue the rose center on the spiral's center. Continue wrapping the larger spiral around the center, securing with glue.

5. Repeat Step 4, continuing to wrap spiral "petals" around the outside of the rose.

6. Glue leaves to the underside of the rose, then glue rose to yellow cupcake base.

7. Glue pom-poms to outer edge of cupcake base. Glue pearl to center of rose.

Finished size: approximately 2½" diameter

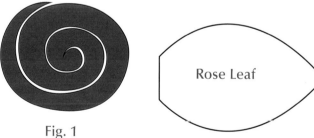

Fig. 1   Rose Leaf

Journal

Shown on page 28.

SHOPPING LIST

- ☐ 5" x 7" stiff cover journal
- ☐ 9" x 12" sheet of black & white houndstooth check felt
- ☐ Scraps of felt (we used green, lime green, blue, light blue, red, hot pink, orange and yellow)
- ☐ Assorted ½" diameter buttons (we used 1 each of blue, pink and green)
- ☐ Yellow embroidery floss
- ☐ Embroidery needle
- ☐ Tracing paper
- ☐ Craft glue

To make the Journal:

1. Mark the outline of the entire journal cover, including its spine, on the tracing paper and cut out. Use the pattern to cut cover from houndstooth check felt. Glue felt to journal, paying special attention to securing the felt edges. Trim if necessary.
2. Trace the patterns onto the tracing paper and cut out. Use the patterns to cut three flowers, three centers and six leaves from felt scraps. Cut one 2" felt circle base.
3. Using a double strand of floss, make a single stitch from the center of the flower, between each of the petals, and back to the center, increasing tension on the floss to gather and pucker the petals.
4. Place a center on a flower. Using 5 strands of yellow floss, sew a button to flower, sewing through all layers. Repeat to make a total of three flowers.
5. Arrange and glue flowers and leaves on base. Glue base to journal.

FInished size: 5" x 7"

Clutch

Shown on page 28.

SHOPPING LIST

- ☐ Pre-made felt clutch (approximately 8" x 12")
- ☐ Scraps of felt (lavender, deep purple and denim blue)
- ☐ Brooch base round pin back (ours is 1" diameter)
- ☐ Tracing paper
- ☐ Low temp glue gun with glue sticks

To make the Clutch:

1. Trace the petal pattern onto the tracing paper and cut out. Use the patterns to cut 12 petals from lavender felt. Cut a 1½" felt circle base.
2. Arrange petals over base like a clock, alternating one petal on top, one petal below. Glue in place.
3. Cut a ½" wide strip of lavender, deep purple, and denim blue felt, each 12" long.
4. Stack the strips. Roll the strips into a tight coil, securing with glue as you go until desired size; trim ends and glue in place.
5. Glue center to daisy.
6. Glue daisy to pin back. Pin the daisy on the clutch.

Finished size: approximately 4½" flower

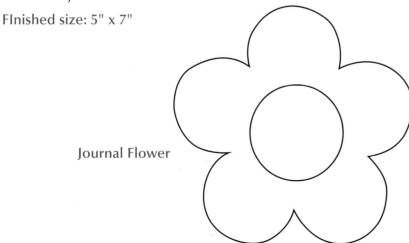

Journal Flower

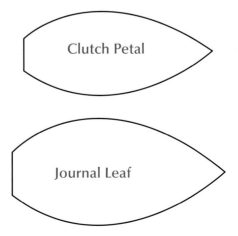

Clutch Petal

Journal Leaf

Floral Wreath

To make the Wreath:

1. Cut gray felt into 4" squares (we used approximately 42).
2. Fold and slit a square as shown in **Fig. 1**. Load the folded square onto outer hoop by threading hoop through slit. Repeat until all squares are loaded or desired fullness is reached.
3. Follow Steps 1-5 on page 30 and make two daisies, using yellow, white, and light green felt. Follow Steps 1-5 on page 27 and make three geraniums, using orange and light green felt. Glue flowers to wreath.

Finished size: approximately 14" diameter

SHOPPING LIST

- ☐ 8" diameter round wooden embroidery hoop
- ☐ ³/₈ yard of 72" wide gray felt
- ☐ 9" x 12" sheet each of yellow, orange, white and light green felt
- ☐ Tracing paper
- ☐ Craft glue

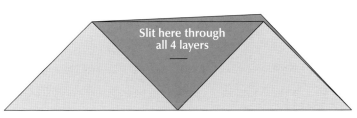

Slit here through all 4 layers

Fig. 1

Embroidery Stitches

Follow the stitch diagrams to bring the needle up
at odd numbers and down at even numbers.

French Knot

Straight Stitch

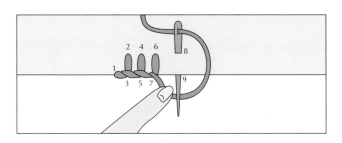

Blanket Stitch

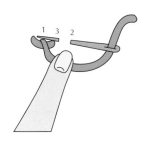

Stem Stitch

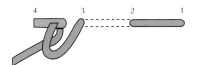

Running Stitch